SI

COUNTRY RECIPES

compiled by
Dorothy Baldock

"Tis an ill cook who cannot
lick his own fingers."
  Romeo and Juliet

SALMON

Index

Cover pictures: *front:* Anne Hathaway's Cottage, Shottery
Back: Chapel Street, Stratford-upon-Avon *by W. W. Quartremain*
Title page: Abbot Reginald's Gateway *by Thomas Tyndale*

White Ladies Pudding

A variation of bread and butter pudding from Worcestershire. The origin of the name is uncertain but could refer to the white habit of local nuns, because convents frequently provided food to travellers.

3 oz desiccated coconut	**Vanilla essence**
5-6 slices of white bread,	**Pinch of salt**
thickly buttered	**2 eggs**
¹/₂ pint milk	**2 oz sugar**

Set oven to 350°F or Mark 4. Butter a 2 to 2¹/₂ pint pie dish and sprinkle thickly with the desiccated coconut. Remove the crusts from the bread and cut into squares or triangles and arrange in the dish. Heat the milk in a saucepan and add a few drops of vanilla essence and the salt. In a bowl, beat the eggs with the sugar, then pour in the milk and stir well. Strain the milk mixture over the bread in the pie dish and leave to soak for 30 minutes. Then place the pie dish in a pan of hot water that comes about half-way up the side and bake for 30 to 40 minutes or until set and browned on top. Serves 4 to 6.

Lord Leycester Hospital, Warwick *by Fred Whitehead*

Warwick Chops

*In this traditional Warwickshire recipe, lamb chops are oven-baked
with onion and chestnuts.*

**8 lamb chops, wiped
  and trimmed
A little seasoned flour
A little oil
A walnut of butter
$^1/_2$ lb onions, peeled and chopped**

**1 oz flour
Salt and black pepper
Pinch English mustard powder
Pinch freshly ground nutmeg
$^3/_4$ to 1 pint well-flavoured
  brown stock or gravy**

1 lb chestnuts, boiled gently for about 5 to 10 minutes, cooled and then peeled

Set oven to 350°F or Mark 4. Heat the oil in a frying pan. Dust the chops with the seasoned flour and fry lightly on both sides to seal. Remove from the pan and place in an ovenproof casserole. Add the butter to any oil remaining in the pan, add the onions and fry until soft and lightly golden. Stir in the flour and seasonings and cook for a few minutes, then gradually stir in the stock or gravy and bring to the boil. Add the chestnuts, simmer for 1 minute, then pour over the chops. Cover and bake for $^3/_4$ to 1 hour. Serve with creamed potatoes and a green vegetable. Serves 4.

Baked Eggs with Herbs

Eggs have always symbolised rebirth, but to the Christian Church they particularly symbolise Christ's Resurrection and the stone rolled away from His Tomb - hence their association with Easter. More practically, poultry begins to lay prolifically at this time, thus providing a farmer's wife with plenty of eggs for nourishing family meals. Originally this Spring supper dish was made with goose eggs, but chicken eggs can be substituted, allowing two per person.

A walnut of butter
6 oz Cheddar cheese, grated
8 eggs
Salt and black pepper

4 heaped tablespoons fresh parsley,
 finely chopped
1 level tablespoon mixed fresh herbs,
 sage, thyme, etc., finely chopped
¼ pint double cream

Set oven to 350°F or Mark 4. Lightly grease a large ovenproof dish with the butter and sprinkle 4 oz of the cheese evenly over the base. Break in the eggs carefully, one at a time, keeping whole and season lightly. Mix the herbs together and sprinkle over, then carefully spoon the cream over the egg yolks and top with the remaining cheese. Bake for 20 minutes or until lightly golden and serve accompanied by crusty bread and butter. Serves 4.

Sherry Cake

A deliciously rich Gloucestershire fruit cake.

4 oz butter, softened   4 oz caster sugar   3 eggs, separated   8 oz flour
Pinch salt   4 oz ground almonds   6 oz currants, sultanas or raisins
2 oz chopped mixed peel   2 oz glacé cherries, halved and tossed in flour
2 oz flaked almonds   Grated rind of half a lemon
1½ to 2 wine glasses of sherry   1 level teaspoon bicarbonate of soda
2 teaspoons vinegar   1 wine glass of sherry

Set oven to 425°F or Mark 7. Cream the butter and sugar together in a bowl until light and fluffy, then add the egg yolks, one at a time, beating well between each addition. Sieve together the flour and salt and stir into the mixture. Stir in the ground almonds, fruit, peel, cherries, flaked almonds and lemon rind, then add the 1½ to 2 glasses of sherry and beat well. Whisk the egg whites until stiff and fold into the mixture. Dissolve the bicarbonate of soda in the vinegar and stir in, mixing thoroughly. Turn the mixture into an 8 inch cake tin lined with buttered greaseproof paper and smooth over the top. Bake for 10 minutes, then lower the heat to 325°F or Mark 3 and bake for a further 1½ to 2 hours, covering the top with a piece of kitchen foil. Remove from the oven and place, still in its tin, on a wire rack. While still hot, spoon over the final wine glass of sherry. Cover with a clean tea towel and leave in the tin to get completely cold before turning out.

Damson, Cinnamon and Apple Fool

Damson trees are a wonderful sight in Spring with their clouds of white blossom and in Autumn there is the bounty of their downy, purple fruits. Mixing damsons and cinnamon together with apples makes a delicious autumn pudding.

$1/2$ lb damsons	2 egg yolks
$1/2$ lb cooking apples	4 tablespoons fresh
2 oz butter, unsalted	white breadcrumbs
4 oz sugar (or more if preferred)	$1/2$ pint double cream
1 teaspoon ground cinnamon	

Wash the damsons and peel, core and thinly slice the apples. Melt the butter in a saucepan, add the fruit and sugar, just cover with water and simmer until the fruit is soft. When cooked, cool and purée the fruit, remove the stones and add more sugar if preferred. Blend in the egg yolks and the breadcrumbs. Return to the saucepan and stir the mixture over a low heat until thickened, then put into a bowl and leave to cool. Meanwhile, whisk the cream lightly and then fold in to the cooled fruit purée, add the cinnamon and mix well. When cold, spoon into individual bowls or sundae glasses and serve. Serves 4.

Pershore Bridge, River Avon *by A. R. Quinton*

Bosworth Jumbles

It is said the original recipe was dropped by Richard III's cook at the Battle of Bosworth Field. The name 'jumble' is derived from 'gemmel' which was an interlaced finger ring, which these biscuits are believed to resemble.

5 oz butter	**10 oz flour**
5 oz sugar	**2 oz ground almonds**
1 egg, beaten	**1 teaspoon grated lemon rind**

Set oven to 350°F or Mark 4. In a bowl, cream the butter and sugar together until light and fluffy, then add the egg. Fold in the flour, ground almonds and finely grated lemon rind to form a soft but firm dough. On a lightly floured surface, roll out the dough with the hands to form a long sausage about the thickness of a middle finger. Cut into pieces approximately 5 inches long and place, well apart, on two well greased baking sheets, carefully curling the pieces into 'S' shapes. Bake for 12 to 15 minutes, then cool on a wire rack.

Asparagus Soup

English asparagus, said to be the finest in the world and grown in the Vale of Evesham, is used to make this delicate and creamy soup.

A good ½ lb asparagus spears, wiped and trimmed
1 pint chicken stock
3 sprigs parsley and a small bayleaf tied together with string

Salt and white pepper
1 teaspoon sugar
1½ oz butter
1½ oz flour
1 pint milk

3 fl.oz double cream

Chop the asparagus into short lengths, reserving a few tips for garnish. Bring the stock to the boil in a saucepan then add the asparagus pieces, herbs, seasoning and sugar. If desired, a few peas or a little chopped spinach can also be added to the stock to enhance the soup's delicate colouring. Bring back to the boil and simmer, covered, for 30 to 40 minutes. Discard the herbs, allow to cool a little, then sieve or purée in a processor or blender. Melt the butter in a clean saucepan and stir in the flour. Add the milk slowly, stirring all the time until the mixture is smooth, then add the asparagus purée, bring to the boil and simmer, stirring, for 2 minutes. Adjust the seasoning, then stir in the cream and heat through, but do not allow to boil. Serve garnished with the reserved asparagus tips. These tips need to be cooked separately for about 10 minutes in a little boiling water to which 2 teaspoons of lemon juice has been added, then drained well. Serves 4 to 6.

Kenilworth Castle from the Ramparts *by W. W. Quatremain*

Pheasant Casserole

A brace of pheasants casseroled with red wine and brandy. A popular shooting party supper dish from Warwickshire.

A brace of pheasant, prepared for cooking	1 carrot, peeled and sliced
A walnut of butter	4-6 small shallots, peeled and left whole
4 rashers back bacon, derinded and chopped	A bay leaf, two sprigs of parsley and a sprig of thyme, tied together with string
1 tablespoon flour	$^1/_2$ pint red wine
Salt and black pepper	2 tablespoons brandy
$^3/_4$ pint chicken stock	6 oz button mushrooms
2 onions, peeled and chopped	

Melt the butter in a frying pan and quickly brown the pheasants on all sides. Remove from the pan and place in a casserole dish. Fry the bacon lightly in the residual butter, then stir in the flour and seasoning. Pour in the stock, stirring all the time. Add the onions, carrot and shallots and bring the mixture to the boil. Pour over the pheasant and add the *bouquet garni* of herbs. Set oven to 325°F or Mark 3. Pour the wine into the casserole, cover and cook for 2$^1/_2$ to 3 hours. Remove the herbs, add the brandy and mushrooms and cook for a further 30 minutes. Serve with creamed potatoes and a green vegetable. Serves 4.

Preserved Pork Shoulder

This farmhouse recipe is a more elaborate alternative to the usual salt-based mixture

A rolled pork shoulder, 2 to 2½ lbs
2 pints cider
¼ pint cider vinegar
1 onion, peeled and quartered,
each stuck with 4 cloves
1 medium carrot, peeled and diced
1 stick celery, trimmed and diced

A thick slice of lemon, optional
A bouquet garni
2 teaspoons whole black peppercorns
½ teaspoon sea salt
1 large apple
Scant ¼ pint cider
Parsley sprigs with fried apple rings

Wipe the pork and place in a deep heatproof dish. Put all the ingredients, except the apple and the ¼ pint cider, into a saucepan, bring gently to the boil, then simmer for 10 minutes. Allow to cool slightly, then pour over the pork. Allow to cool completely, then cover, put in a cool place and leave for 2 to 3 days, turning the pork regularly. Remove the pork and dry with kitchen paper. Discard the liquid. Set oven to 325°F or Mark 3. Peel, core and roughly chop the apple. Place the pork in a casserole, surround with the chopped apple, then pour over the ¼ pint cider. Cover and cook for 2 hours. Turn up the oven to 400°F or Mark 6. Remove the pork, place in a roasting tin and return to the oven for 10 to 15 minutes to crisp the outside. Allow to cool completely. Serve sliced, garnished with parsley sprigs and apple rings accompanied by Mustard Sauce. Serves 4.

Fourteen

Malvern Pudding

This is a fruit version of Hasty Pudding, one of the earliest of all old English puddings and so called because it was very quickly made.

1 lb stewed apples	**1 pint milk, warmed to blood heat**
3 oz butter	**2 oz caster sugar**
1½ oz flour	**1 teaspoon ground cinnamon**

Set oven to 350ºF or Mark 4. First, peel and core the apples, slice and put into a saucepan with just a little water. Bring to the boil and boil until the apples are reduced to a pulp. Melt half the butter in a saucepan, stir in the flour, then gradually add the milk, stirring continually until the mixture is thick and smooth. Spoon layers of apple and the 'custard' into a buttered 2 to 2½ pint pie dish, finishing with a layer of 'custard'. Dot with the remaining butter. Mix the sugar and cinnamon together and sprinkle over the pudding. Bake for 20 minutes, then place under a hot grill for 1 to 2 minutes to brown the top. Serves 4 to 6.

Northamptonshire Seed Cake

A plain cake flavoured with nutmeg and caraway seeds which was traditionally served at sheep shearing time.

8 oz butter	**8 oz flour**
8 oz caster sugar	**¹/₂ teaspoon baking powder**
4 eggs	**1 teaspoon ground nutmeg**
	1 oz caraway seeds

Set oven to 350°F or Mark 4. Cream the butter and sugar together in a bowl until light and fluffy. Place the eggs in a bowl set over a saucepan of hot water and whisk until fluffy, then whisk into the butter mixture. Sift the flour and baking powder together and fold into the mixture, together with the nutmeg. Add the caraway seeds and combine well. Turn into a greased and lined 8 inch round cake tin and smooth over the top. Bake for 1¹/₂ to 2 hours, covering the top with a piece of kitchen foil if it appears to be browning too quickly. Cool in the tin for 5 minutes, then turn out on to a wire rack.

Sulgrave Manor: George Washington's Birthplace *by David Neave*

Stuffed Savoury Pancakes

*This Warwickshire recipe can be served either as a supper dish or
as a first course or starter.*

½ lb cooked chicken or lean
   ham, finely chopped, or
   a mixture of both
1 oz butter
2 oz mushrooms, wiped
   and sliced

1 small onion, peeled and finely sliced
½ pint prepared white sauce,
   well-seasoned and rather thick
1 pint prepared pancake batter
Lard for frying
2 oz grated Cheddar cheese

Place the meat in a bowl. Melt the butter in a frying pan and lightly fry the
mushrooms. Drain well and add to the meat. Fry the onion in the remaining butter
until soft and add to the meat and mushrooms. Stir in the white sauce and combine
well, adjusting the seasoning if necessary. Turn into a saucepan and heat through
until almost boiling. Using the pancake batter make the first pancake, frying it in
lard. Place a tablespoon of the white sauce mixture on one half and roll up tightly.
Place on a hot dish. Make the remainder of the pancakes in the same way, placing
them side by side on the dish. Sprinkle over the cheese and place under a hot grill
for 1 to 2 minutes until the cheese is melted and bubbling and the pancakes heated
through. Serves 4 to 6.

Banbury Cakes

These oval cakes date back to Tudor days and were originally sold around the town from special lidded baskets, wrapped in white cloths to keep them warm.

1 lb prepared puff pastry	**2 oz mixed peel**
2 oz butter, melted	**4 oz demerara sugar**
4 oz raisins	**1 level teaspoon mixed spice**
4 oz currants	**Egg white and caster sugar, for topping**

Set oven to 425°F or Mark 7. Mix the melted butter, fruit, peel, sugar and spice together in a bowl, combining well. Roll out the pastry on a lightly floured surface and, using a saucer, cut into about 16 circles. Divide the fruit mixture evenly between them, then dampen the edges of the pastry circles and draw up into the centre, sealing well. Turn over and, with the hands, gently form the cakes into ovals, then press down very gently with a rolling pin. Make 3 diagonal cuts across the top of each cake, then brush with egg white and sprinkle with sugar. Place on lightly greased baking trays and bake for 15 to 20 minutes or until golden. Serve slightly warm. Makes about 16 cakes.

Compton Wynyates *by W. W. Quatremain*

Port Wine Jelly

An elegant, richly flavoured dinner party dessert that was particularly popular in Victorian days; a Warwickshire recipe.

2 oz gelatine crystals
8 tablespoons cold water
1½ pints port wine
¼ pint water
1 lb blackcurrant jam or jelly

3 teaspoons lemon juice and 2-inch twist
of very finely pared lemon rind
A pinch ground cinnamon
A pinch freshly ground nutmeg
3 oz caster sugar
½ pint double cream

Soak the gelatine in 2 tablespoons of the cold water in a bowl until spongy, then add the remaining 6 tablespoons of water and stir VERY gently. Reserving ½ pint port, put the remainder, together with all the other ingredients except the cream, in a large saucepan and stir gently. Add the gelatine and simmer over a low heat until it reaches just below boiling point. Remove from the heat and stir in the reserved port. Rinse out a 2 pint jelly mound in cold water and strain the port mixture into it. Allow to cool a little, then chill in the refrigerator until fully set; allow about 6 to 7 hours. Whip the cream until it stands up in peaks. Turn the jelly out on to a serving dish (if it sticks, dip the mould briefly in hot water) and decorate with piped stars or rosettes of cream. Serve with extra cream, if desired. Serves 6 to 8. If preferred, the jelly can be made in and served from a decorative serving dish.

Pickled Mushrooms

Mushrooms, morning-picked from the fields, are delicious pickled.

8 oz mushrooms, wiped and trimmed
(button ones, left whole, are best)
A little salt
$\frac{1}{4}$ teaspoon cayenne pepper
A squeeze of lemon juice

$\frac{1}{2}$ pint white vinegar
2 level teaspoons pickling spice
2 sprigs parsley
1 small bayleaf
A little chopped fresh parsley, to garnish

Place the mushrooms in a bowl, sprinkle over a little salt and leave to stand in a cool place for 3 to 4 hours. Drain well and pat dry with kitchen paper. Place in a saucepan that has been rinsed out in cold water and sprinkle over the cayenne pepper and lemon juice. Place the saucepan over a VERY low heat to set the mushroom juices running and shake gently from time to time. Put the vinegar, pickling spice, parsley sprigs and bayleaf in another saucepan, bring to the boil, then simmer for 10 to 15 minutes. Strain the vinegar over the mushrooms. Bring to the boil, then remove from the heat. Transfer the mushrooms and liquid into a heatproof bowl and allow to cool completely. Finally, pour into a clean, dry glass container and cover. Keep in a cool, dark place for 2 to 3 days before using. To serve, place the drained mushrooms in a dish, sprinkle with a little chopped parsley and serve as an accompaniment to cold meat, poultry or ham.

Cider-baked Fish

Cider and fish make a pleasant combination in this Worcestershire recipe.

4 cod or other white fish steaks	**1½ oz butter**
A little butter	**1½ oz flour**
4 sprigs parsley	**Milk**
Salt and black pepper	**1 tablespoon fresh, chopped parsley**
½ pint cider	**Parsley sprigs, for garnish**

Set oven to 350°F or Mark 4. Wipe the fish steaks, place in an ovenproof casserole and season lightly. Dot each steak with a little butter and place a parsley sprig on top. Pour over the cider, cover and bake for 20 minutes. Reserving the liquid, carefully remove the fish steaks, drain well, place on a heated serving dish and keep warm. Melt the butter in a saucepan and stir in the flour. Strain the fish liquid and make up to about ¾ pint with the milk. Add to the flour mixture, a little at a time, stirring continually until the sauce boils and thickens. Season, stir in the chopped parsley and pour into a warmed sauceboat. Serve the fish steaks, garnished with parsley sprigs, with creamed potatoes, green peas and grilled tomatoes and with the sauce served separately. Serves 4.

High Tea Cake

High tea was a hearty farmhouse meal that began with cold meats or pies with salad and bread and butter and progressed through scones, teabread and jelly or trifle to finish up with a rich, fruit-filled cake.

5 oz butter	A good $\frac{1}{4}$ pint milk
6 level tablespoons golden syrup	8 oz flour
8 oz raisins	Pinch salt
8 oz currants	$1\frac{1}{2}$ teaspoons mixed spice
8 oz sultanas	1 teaspoon ground nutmeg
4 oz chopped dates	2 eggs, beaten
Finely grated rind of a lemon	$\frac{1}{2}$ level teaspoon bicarbonate of soda

Set oven to 325°F or Mark 3. Place the butter, syrup, fruit, lemon rind and milk in a saucepan and heat gently until the butter is melted. Simmer for 5 minutes, stirring gently. Allow to cool. Sieve together the flour, salt and spices into a bowl and make a well in the centre. Beat the eggs lightly together, pour into the well but do not stir in. Add the bicarbonate of soda to the cooled butter mixture, pour into the well over the eggs and mix thoroughly. Turn into a 7 to 8 inch cake tin lined with buttered greaseproof paper and smooth over the top. Bake for $1\frac{3}{4}$ to 2 hours, covering the top with kitchen foil if it appears to be browning too quickly. Cool in the tin for 10 minutes, then turn out on to a wire rack. Remove the paper when the cake is cold.

Cottages at Little Comberton *by A. R. Quinton*

Dumpsie Dearie Jam

This is an old country recipe from the Gloucestershire border which makes use of windfall apples, pears and plums.

2 lbs pears   2 lbs cooking apples   2 lbs plums
Grated zest and juice of 1 lemon   Pinch ground cloves
$^1/_2$ oz fresh ginger root, bruised   5 lbs sugar

Peel and core the pears and apples. Halve and stone the plums. Put all the fruit into a large pan with the lemon zest and juice, the ground cloves and bruised ginger root. Simmer very gently until the fruit is soft; if it starts to stick to the pan add a little water. Stir in the sugar until completely dissolved and then bring to the boil. Boil rapidly (a good rolling boil) for about 15 to 20 minutes until setting point is reached, testing for set on a cold saucer. Pour into warm, sterilised jars, cover and seal.

Oat Bread

An old Warwickshire farmhouse recipe, this sweet bread contains no yeast, but uses baking powder as its raising agent. It develops a cake-like consistency when baked and is delicious served spread with butter.

³/₄ pint milk	4 teaspoons baking powder
4 oz porridge or rolled oats	6 oz caster sugar
12 oz flour	1 egg, beaten
1 teaspoon salt	¹/₂ oz butter, melted

Scald the milk by pouring into a saucepan and heating gently until bubbles begin to appear round the rim of the milk. Then pour over the oats in a bowl, stir lightly and leave to cool. In another bowl, sieve together the flour, salt and baking powder, then stir in the sugar. Beat in the egg and melted butter, then stir in the oat mixture and combine well; it will be the consistency of very thick porridge. Turn into a well buttered 2 lb loaf tin and leave to stand for 15 to 20 minutes. Set the oven to 350°F or Mark 4. When proved, bake for 1¹/₂ hours. After about ¹/₂ hour cover the top with a piece of VERY lightly buttered kitchen foil to prevent the top from browning too much. Turn out on to a wire rack to cool. Serve thickly sliced and spread with plenty of butter. Oat Bread is not a long-term keeper.

In Jephson Gardens, Leamington Spa *by W. W. Quatremain*

Leamingtons

This flat sponge cake topped with chocolate icing and coconut and cut into squares is a Warwickshire recipe.

2 eggs	**4 oz flour**
4 oz butter	**1 teaspoon baking powder**
4 oz caster sugar	**Chocolate glacé icing**
2-3 tablespoons desiccated coconut	

Set oven to 375°F or Mark 5. Break the eggs into a bowl set over a pan of hot water and beat lightly. In a bowl, cream the butter and sugar together then gradually beat in the eggs. Sift the flour and baking powder together and fold into the mixture. Turn the mixture into a greased and base lined 8 inch square tin 2 inches deep and bake for 15 minutes until golden, well risen and springy to the touch. Allow to cool in the tin, then cut into squares. Coat each square with chocolate glacé icing and sprinkle with the desiccated coconut. Makes about 9 squares.

Hunting Pudding

Also known as Leicestershire Pudding, there are a number of variations of this recipe, which dates back at least to the 18th century. As well as being served as part of a hearty meal after a day's hunting, this pudding was also sliced cold and taken as a snack to be eaten on the hunting field.

½ lb seedless raisins	1 teaspoon grated lemon rind
4 oz flour	1 teaspoon ground nutmeg
4 oz shredded suet	1 fl. oz brandy
2 eggs, beaten	Milk

In a bowl, mix together the raisins, flour and suet, then stir in the eggs, lemon rind, nutmeg and brandy, combining well. Add sufficient milk to make a stiff mixture and spoon into a well buttered 1½ to 2 pint pudding basin. Smooth over the top and cover with buttered greaseproof paper and kitchen foil and seal. Place in a saucepan with sufficient boiling water to come half-way up the basin, cover and steam for 4 hours, adding more water as necessary. Turn out of the basin on to a warm serving dish and serve with brandy-flavoured whipped cream or custard. Serves 4.

Traditionally this pudding was boiled in a well floured cloth, making it ball shaped, in the style of an old-fashioned Christmas Pudding.

Chicken in Mushroom Sauce

An appetising and practical way to cook a chicken that is too old and tough for successful roasting.

A 3½ lb to 4 lb prepared chicken	**Salt**
1 onion, peeled and quartered	**A thick slice lemon, optional**
1 large carrot, peeled and diced	**2 teaspoons vinegar**
1 stick celery, wiped and diced	**1 oz butter**
3 sprigs of parsley and	**1 teaspoon lemon juice**
** 1 bayleaf tied together with string**	**6 oz mushrooms, wiped and sliced**
6 peppercorns	**2 oz flour**
2 cloves	**Chopped fresh parsley, to garnish**

Place the chicken, vegetables, herbs, seasonings and lemon, if desired, in a large saucepan and almost cover with cold water. Add the vinegar and bring to the boil. Cover and simmer for 2 to 2 ½ hours. Remove the chicken from the liquid and drain well, reserving the chicken stock. Joint the chicken or keep whole, as preferred, place on a heated serving dish and keep warm. Melt the butter in a saucepan, add the lemon juice and the mushrooms and fry lightly. Stir in the flour and fry for a further 2 minutes. Strain the stock and stir into the mushroom mixture a little at a time. Bring to the boil and boil, stirring, for 5 minutes. Pour over the chicken and garnish wish parsley. Serve with boiled potatoes, carrots and a green vegetable. Serves 4 to 6.

Malvern Apple Pudding

A steamed pudding containing finely chopped Russet apples,
currants and brandy.

4 oz butter   **4 Russet eating apples, peeled,**
4 oz sugar   **cored and finely chopped**
2 eggs, beaten   **Grated rind of 1 lemon**
4 oz flour   **1 teaspoon lemon juice**
Pinch of salt   **1 oz currants or sultanas**
2-3 tablespoons brandy

Beat the butter and sugar together in a bowl until light and fluffy, then beat in the eggs. Sift the flour and salt together and fold into the mixture, then add the apples, lemon rind and juice, fruit and brandy. Combine well together and turn into a buttered $2\frac{1}{2}$ pint pudding basin. Cover with greaseproof paper and kitchen foil and seal. Place in a saucepan, pour in sufficient boiling water to come half way up the side of the basin and steam for $1\frac{1}{2}$ to 2 hours, topping up the water when necessary. Turn out the pudding on to a warm serving dish and serve with custard, cream or brandy sauce. Serves 4 to 6.

From the Malvern Hills *by A. R. Quinton*

Shy Cake

*A plain cake containing ground rice and flavoured with lemon
and ginger. This is a Warwickshire recipe.*

4 oz butter	1 teaspoon ground ginger
6 oz demerara sugar	1 teaspoon baking powder
4 oz flour	1 teaspoon lemon juice
8 oz ground rice	2 eggs, beaten

Set oven to 350°F or Mark 4. In a bowl, cream the butter and sugar together until fluffy. Sift together the flour, ground rice, ginger and baking powder. Add the lemon juice to the creamed mixture, then add the flour mixture and the beaten eggs alternately, beating well between each addition. Turn into a well buttered and base lined 8 inch round cake tin and smooth the top. Bake for 1 to $1\frac{1}{2}$ hours, covering the top with a piece of kitchen foil if it appears to be browning too quickly. Cool in the tin for 5 minutes, then turn out on to a wire rack.

Stuffed Lamb Rounds

Breast of lamb is an economical cut that combines deliciously with a forcemeat stuffing. This farmhouse recipe comes from Worcestershire.

2 lb breast of lamb, skinned and boned
A little oil
1 shallot or small onion, peeled and chopped
2 oz streaky bacon, derinded and chopped
3 oz fresh breadcrumbs

1 dessertspoon fresh, chopped parsley
1 teaspoon fresh, chopped mint
Grated rind of half a lemon
1 egg, beaten
Salt and black pepper
Pinch of dry English mustard
A walnut of butter

Remove any excess fat from the lamb. Heat the oil in a frying pan and fry the onion until soft but not brown, then add the bacon pieces and fry lightly. Allow to cool. Set oven to 350°F or Mark 4. In a bowl, combine the onion and bacon with the breadcrumbs, herbs and lemon rind and stir in sufficient beaten egg to bind the mixture. Lightly season the lamb, spread with the stuffing and roll up tightly, securing at intervals with kitchen string. Cut into rounds between the string and place them flat in an ovenproof casserole. Season with salt, pepper and mustard powder and dot with butter. Cover and cook for 1 to 1½ hours. To serve, remove the string and serve the rounds with boiled potatoes, carrots and peas, accompanied by thin gravy. Serves 4.

Thirty-five

A Gossip at Long Compton *by Fred Whitehead*

Grandmother's Cheesecake

Cheesecakes made with fresh curd were popular farmhouse fare.
This Warwickshire recipe is made with cream cheese.

8 oz prepared shortcrust pastry	**Grated rind of half a lemon**
8 oz cream cheese	**2 teaspoons lemon juice**
2 oz sugar	**Pinch of salt**
1 egg, beaten	**$\frac{1}{2}$ teaspoon ground nutmeg**
2 oz currants	**1 oz butter, softened**

A little milk

Set oven to 350°F or Mark 4. Roll out the pastry on a lightly floured surface and use to line a lightly greased 8 inch flan tin, trimming the edges neatly. In a bowl, mix together the cheese and the sugar, then add the egg, beating well to combine thoroughly. Stir in the currants, lemon rind and juice, salt and nutmeg, then turn the mixture into the flan case and smooth over the top. Cut the butter into thin slices and use to dot the top of the filling. Brush the rim of the pastry with a little milk and bake for 35 to 40 minutes until golden. Serve cold, accompanied by pouring cream. Serves 4.

Originally this cheesecake was made with warmed milk (or half milk, half cream) curdled with rennet. The whey was then drained off and the curd used for the cheesecake filling.

Pork with Oranges

Oranges were once a more popular accompaniment to pork than apples are today.

2½ to 3 lb leg or loin of pork	Salt and black pepper
A walnut of butter	3 to 4 fl. oz water
1 small onion, peeled and very finely chopped	2 oranges
1 fresh sage leaf, finely chopped	1 tablespoon redcurrant jelly
	2 fl. oz sherry

Set oven to 350°F or Mark 4. Wipe the pork with kitchen paper. Melt the butter in a frying pan and fry the onion until soft. Transfer to a roasting tin. Season the pork with the sage and pepper and place on top of the onions. Pour the water round and roast for about 1½ to 2 hours. Meanwhile, grate the peel from 1 orange, then squeeze and strain the juice. Cut the other orange into 6 or 8 segments, without peeling. Remove the pork from the oven and sprinkle over it the orange peel, pressing down lightly with a palette knife. Add the orange juice to the juices in the roasting tin, together with the redcurrant jelly and sherry. Place the orange segments round the pork, return to the oven and cook for a further 20 to 30 minutes. Place the pork on a heated serving dish and surround with the orange segments. Pour the pan juices into a sauceboat. Serve with roast potatoes and a selection of vegetables. Serves 4 to 6.

Coventry Godcakes

The triangular shape of these cakes and the three slits across the top are said to represent the Holy Trinity, though presumably on those occasions the rum was definitely optional.

8 oz prepared puff pastry　　**2 teaspoons rum, optional**
4 oz mincemeat　　**1 egg white**
Caster sugar

Set oven to 425°F or Mark 7. Roll out the pastry thinly on a lightly floured surface and cut into 4 inch squares, then cut each square in half on the diagonal to make two triangles. Mix the mincemeat with the rum, if desired, and place spoonfuls on half of the triangles. Cover each one with another triangle, moistening the edges with a little water and pressing down firmly to seal. Beat the egg white lightly. Cut three slits in each cake with a very sharp knife, then brush with egg white. Sprinkle with caster sugar and place on a greased baking sheet. Bake for 15 minutes or until well risen and golden. Cool on a wire rack and eat as fresh as possible.

Tewkesbury Saucer Batters

These individual fruit-filled, two-sided pancakes are delicious with whatever variety of fruit may be in season to make a stewed purée.

2 eggs, separated	½ pint milk
3 oz flour	Stewed soft fruit, apples, plums,
Pinch of salt	raspberries, etc., as available
1 oz sugar	Icing sugar, for sifting

Set oven to 400°F or Mark 6. Separate the eggs. Mix together in a bowl the flour, salt and sugar. Make a well in the centre and add the egg yolks and the milk. Beat to a smooth batter. Whisk the egg whites until they will just hold their shape and fold in. Butter 8 to 10 large ovenproof saucers and divide the batter between them. Bake for 15 to 20 minutes. Place half the batters on warmed serving plates and top with the stewed soft fruit. Place the remaining batters on top of each base and serve at once, sprinkled (if desired) with a little sifted icing sugar. Serves 4 to 5. If preferred, large batters can be made by using ovenproof plates and the batters then served cut into portions.

King John's Bridge, Tewkesbury *by A. R. Quinton*

Warwick Pudding

A steamed pudding containing dried figs and flavoured with ginger.

4 tablespoons ginger wine	1 oz gelatine
2 oz dried figs, trimmed and very finely chopped	4 tablespoons water
$\frac{1}{2}$ pint milk	$\frac{1}{2}$ pint double cream
3 egg yolks	1 oz preserved ginger, very finely chopped
2 oz caster sugar	Whipped cream for decoration

Overnight, soak the chopped figs in the ginger wine. Next day, drain off the ginger wine from the figs and set both aside. Put the milk into a saucepan and heat until almost boiling. Whisk the egg yolks and sugar together and stir into the milk, combining well. Stir gently over a low heat until the custard is creamy, then allow to cool. Put the gelatine in a cup with the water and stand in a saucepan of hot water, stirring gently until the gelatine has dissolved and is syrupy. Stir the melted gelatine into the ginger wine and set aside until lukewarm. Whip the cream until it stands up in soft peaks. Stir the gelatine into the custard, then combine together the custard and the cream, whisking well. Allow the mixture to cool and thicken, then stir in the chopped ginger. Add the drained figs to the mixture, stir lightly and pour into a glass serving bowl. Stir lightly and leave in a cool place to set. Decorate with rosettes of whipped cream. Serve chilled with pouring cream. Serves 4 to 6.

Spicy Stewed Pears

Ripe pears picked off the tree are a real taste of Autumn. This adaptation of an old Worcestershire recipe combines another autumn fruit - blackberries - with the pears. Comice pears are ideal for this dish but are not essential.

6 pears	**$^1/_4$ - $^1/_2$ pint sweet cider**
$^1/_2$ lb blackberries	**1 teaspoon dried mixed spice**
$^1/_4$ - $^1/_2$ pint red wine	**$^1/_2$ - 1 teaspoon ground ginger**

Wash the blackberries well and peel the pears and leave whole. Put the fruits together into a saucepan, pour on the red wine and add the mixed spice and ground ginger. Gently poach the fruit over a low heat until tender. Remove the pears, cut each one in half, carefully remove the cores and return to the pan. Now just cover with sweet cider, bring to the boil and boil rapidly until the liquid is reduced and syrupy. Serve with whipped cream. Serves 6.

Shakespeare's Birthplace, Stratford-upon-Avon *by W. W. Quatremain*

Wafers

*Light and crispy wafers date back to Shakespeare's time and, like the later brandy
snaps, were a popular sweetmeat to be enjoyed on market days and at fairs.
Traditionally, they should be eaten hot.*

4 oz flour   2 oz butter, softened
Pinch salt   ¹/₂ fl. oz double cream
1 level tablespoon clear honey

Set oven to 300°F or Mark 2. Lightly butter a baking sheet. Sieve the flour and
salt together into a bowl and rub in the butter until the mixture resembles fine
breadcrumbs. Stir in the cream and honey. Roll out thinly on a lightly floured
surface and cut into small rounds. Place the wafers on the baking sheet, allowing
plenty of room between each one and bake for 15 to 20 minutes until crisp.
Transfer to a wire rack to cool.

Farmhouse Pudding

This layered and steamed meat pudding is also known as Wellingborough Hough and Dough Cake - 'hough' being another name for shin of beef.

1 lb shin of beef, finely diced
2 medium onions, peeled and chopped
1 to 2 tablespoons cooking oil
  or 1 oz dripping
3 medium carrots, peeled and grated

1 dessertspoon chopped fresh parsley
1 oz flour
³/₄ pint beef stock
Salt and black pepper
1 lb prepared suet pastry

Mix the meat and onion together. Heat the oil or dripping in a frying pan and fry the meat mixture until brown, then stir in the carrots, parsley and flour. Gradually add the stock and cook, stirring, until the mixture is thick and boiling. Season. Grease a 2 pint pudding basin. Roll out the pastry on a lightly floured surface and cut a circle that will fit the bottom of the basin. Place a layer of meat mixture over this, then add another circle of pastry, continuing to fill the basin with alternate layers, finishing with a circle of pastry. Cover the pudding with greaseproof paper and kitchen foil and seal. Steam for 1 to 1¹/₂ hours, topping up the water when necessary. Serve direct from the basin with boiled potatoes and a green vegetable. Serves 4 to 6.

Gooseberry Tart

The first gooseberries of the season, especially when baked in a tart or pie, are traditionally served on Whit Sunday, making a pudding that has always been particularly popular in the county of Warwickshire. The elderflower heads give a delicate Muscat flavour to the fruit.

1 to 1½ lbs gooseberries, topped and tailed, then rinsed and drained

1 level tablespoon sugar	**2 eggs, beaten**
1 or 2 elderflower heads, rinsed	**¼ pint double cream**
and the stems removed	**4 tablespoons clear honey**

8 oz prepared shortcrust pastry

Place the gooseberries, sugar and elderflower heads in a saucepan with a little water and simmer until the gooseberries are very soft. Remove the elderflower heads, sieve the gooseberries or purée in a processor or blender, allow to cool and then stir in the eggs. Fold the cream and honey together and stir into the gooseberry mixture. Set oven to 400°F or Mark 6. Roll out the pastry on a lightly floured surface and use to line a lightly greased 8 inch flan dish or pie plate, trimming the edges neatly. Pour the gooseberry mixture into the case and bake for 30 to 40 minutes or until the filling is golden. Place on a wire rack and allow to cool before serving, either on its own or with pouring cream as an accompaniment. Serves 4.

METRIC CONVERSIONS

The weights, measures and oven temperatures used in the preceding recipes can be easily converted to their metric equivalents. The conversions listed below are only approximate, having been rounded up or down as may be appropriate.

Weights

Avoirdupois	Metric
1 oz.	just under 30 grams
4 oz. (¼ lb.)	app. 115 grams
8 oz. (½ lb.)	app. 230 grams
1 lb.	454 grams

Liquid Measures

Imperial	Metric
1 tablespoon (liquid only)	20 millilitres
1 fl. oz.	app. 30 millilitres
1 gill (¼ pt.)	app. 145 millilitres
½ pt.	app. 285 millilitres
1 pt.	app. 570 millilitres
1 qt.	app. 1.140 litres

Oven Temperatures

	°Fahrenheit	Gas Mark	°Celsius
Slow	300	2	150
	325	3	170
Moderate	350	4	180
	375	5	190
	400	6	200
Hot	425	7	220
	450	8	230
	475	9	240

Flour as specified in these recipes refers to plain flour unless otherwise described.